The Cartographer's Melancholy

The Cartographer's
Melancholy

David Axelrod

Winner of the Spokane Prize for Poetry

Lynx House Press
Spokane, WA

Acknowledgments

The author wishes to thank the editors of the following publications in which some of the poems in this book first appeared: *Blue Mesa Review, Boulevard, Fine Madness, Hotel Amerika, Kerf, Louisville Review, Prosadia, Quarterly West,* and *Samsara.*

The entirety of "Chronicles of the Withering State," first appeared as a chapbook, under the same title, published by Ice River Press, 2004.

Book design: Joelean Copeland
Cover design: Joanna Darlington
Cover art: *Plowed Under* © Kasey Keeler

ISBN: 978-0-89924-160-9

Cataloging-in-Publication Data available from the Library of Congress upon request.

Lynx House Press books are distributed by the University Of Washington Press, Box 359570, Seattle, WA 98195

In memory: Douglas Myers and Walter Pavlich

Contents

III

IV

V

I

There is, one might say, a kind of untouchable reserve of incomprehensibility in certain things that the calculations of human intelligence are capable neither of removing nor of diminishing, but only of arranging this way or that, sometimes leaving everything in a half-light, at another time illuminating certain points at the expense of others, which are then submerged by a darkness even deeper...

—Antoine Cournot

TILED MOSAIC

At the city gate,
in the damp shadow of limestone
quarried first by slaves and later
by zealots, he knelt. Holy site piled upon

wreckage of holy site. A vertical profile
of conquests. In this way, he found the *Judería*,
below the ruins of the Roman bridge—its vandalized
streets and baths full of leaves and broken glass.

*

After making love, he asked to photograph her
staring straight into the lens, where the mirror deflected
the gaze of his squinted eye. A prank they would play
on whomever might later remark about

that strange expression on her face.
She felt ill-at-ease in that city,
intimidated by graffiti painted on walls.
She asked, *Should anything so frank be framed?*

*

Bowing in the urine-stench of shadows below wrought-iron,
he uncovered the six-pointed star of his namesake—
bright chips of glass inlaid into paving stones. An empty street,
No less claustrophobic now

than during the interregnum, when anarchy erupted
like a virus in the blood. This star. This vertigo
of infinitely repeating patterns
designed to trick the eye.

*

Not the scent of horses, but of Christians.
The tripartite reconstruction of La Sinagoga de Santa Maria la Blanca—
an absurd name, for what was, briefly, a military stable,
and is now empty, except of light,

and this oddity: the Moroccan who followed the couple
into the sanctuary, half-hidden
behind columns near the door, who raises his hands
to cover his face as he prays.

*

In my city, men pass in the street, walking in such pain and haste,
color has drained from their faces. They are the foulest ghosts
alive, flinching from the intimate touch of morning air.
When I meet their eyes, they quickly look elsewhere.

No city claims me as its son. I've wandered instead
half a lifetime in slovenly forests, and because of this am condemned.
I don't know my neighbors' names, who is their god,
nor who is my mine.

*

His daughter turned just that one time from the window
through which the light of her father's studio glowed,
and all of her yet-unconscious being saturated his—
a moment's glance. Three centuries later,

in the same city, a performance of a four-hour-long trio
for piano, cello, and flute, homage to a friend the composer betrayed.
They quarreled about the deconstruction of the human form—
the grotesque canvasses hanging there on the walls, listening.

*

It's only two day's train ride to the besieged city.
Unable to breathe in the empty coach, he closes his eyes,
and panicking, tries to see that girl's face again in half-profile,
a precise and unambiguous oval of light,

the scent of oleanders, the memory of last things,
sanctuary carved from darkness. The train from Nijmegen
approaches a bridge over the Rhine that tyrants marched
and retreated across twice in two-hundred years.

*

She disliked that image of herself flushed with orgasm,
her naked shoulders leaning against bright whitewashed walls.
A strange expression on her face! Ill-at-ease in that city,
she said, *Anything so frank should be framed?*

Beneath the city 25,000 years ago, a hunter carved the intaglio
of an ibex on a cave wall, and of himself, drawing a bow.
The ashes of the fire, by whose light he worked, resist
oblivion: a black circle in the corner of the grotto.

*

At Rita's funeral, the Padre described heaven
as Disneyland! Mourners filed forward to take Communion,
because—reversing the polar directions of our lives
we are unable to accept death except in the abstract.

How then shall bodies hoisted from wells saturate us?
Or the terror of a shrieking child caught in the cross-fire of militias?
Or an entire nation stinking of rotted flesh?
At what point will the abstract no longer contradict the real?

*

In ditch water.
The refugee road.
The ruined city it takes just two days to reach by train.
Communion—the lowest form of vaudeville, our art of the unspeakable.

A few pennies to taint a child's tongue.
On each coin, in profile, the tyrant's face.
A jittery young man leaves a package under a table in a café.
In crowds, traffic, sewer-stench. Windows full of yellow dresses.

*

As Beatrice Martín danced, he ached with lust
for the elemental death she enacted on the dark stage.
Singer, guitarists, dumbfounded audience of middle-aged men—
in each of the dying, the green pulp of his bones re-awakening.

One man shouted *Olé*! because there is a variety of torment
so dire we understand our sins cannot be forgiven
by any formula, least of all by forgetting
we are lost, but no less dazzled.

II

And yet the fear! How people do always carry their own enemy, however powerless he is, within themselves.

—Franz Kafka

CHRONICLES OF THE WITHERING STATE

A Minor Contemporary (On the Editor of the Chronicles*)*

To contextualize his effort, curators include this pastel sketch by one of the man's mistresses, depicting an intimacy and animal warmth he failed in every case to bring forth. The same failure presents itself in our own lives: how best to bring forth our mortal forms? Her full breasts, thick hips, the fall of long hair across the clavicle that must have just shuddered like a wing. Or her lover, who is nothing but a thin line uncoiling beside her, stretching toward the border of their bed's heat. In this we recognize that we are, as we fear, a near-emptiness. Our bodies these brief radiancies only darkness defines the edges of.

1 *Preludium 1984*

We just finished wood-cutting and were hauling the last split cord down an aspen-lined lane. At the squatters' camp where the road divides, they sat in the door of the concession stand scavenged from the fairgrounds: a ferocious old woman and a man with short legs, hunched over a smoky fire. Miles overhead, mare's tails streamed east ahead of the season's first storm. Larches drizzled gold in the foothills. And our radio blared its reports: a Marine invasion, an economy booming somewhere, another farmer had shot himself dead in acres of priceless wheat.

2 The Consolations of Reverend Malthus

The same spectacle every autumn: flies swarming at warm windowpanes. One by one they starve, lose their grip, spiral to the sill, buzz, and grow still. In this we acknowledge the approach of winter, famine, pre-destination. Events that reveal elemental law. Our error, however, is our faith in consolation. We insist fate may be located in examples of blind and ordinary persistence, but only because we believe we are exempt from similar misperceptions. We assume that we will close this gap that perplexed the flies, and fall through the glass barrier that separates us from kinder gods, those who remain invisible and more restrained than any others we know.

3 *First Interrogation*

Q: Is it lightness, as of steam leaping into air from plowed
    fields?
A: What is coming bulges, a gloaming under pines.

Q: Does it make your knees ache?
A: It is not without weight.

Q: Is it unambiguous, upright?
A: It speaks with a pipsqueak's voice.

Q: Can you narrow yourself to a filament along which jolts will
    pass?
A: Yes, one would think to get away.

Q: Mottled as a pomegranate?
A: No, it has already dropped its seeds.

Q: Sour as a dead man's mouth?
A: Meaty as a tumor and sleek as a rat.

Q: Is it the scent a nightmare makes?
A: Infection already pins down the horizon.

Q: Has it come alive in your throat?
A: No, much deeper, in the chambers beneath my ribs.

4 *Of the Miraculous*

Respectable thinkers proclaim respectable endings: elegant, reasoned finales of the Spirit of the Age, of a theory realized, and, of course, of the moral clarity of victors. And yet, we are aware not much ends in so tidy a way. The Respectable Book closes with a sigh....One morning an ant scuttles across the table top where the Pacifist has been thinking. He glances up from the impure page, from what he wished might emerge. The Miraculous? The ant was going another direction, hurrying after a mission in the dark span between the table and the paneling, its antennae leading the way, hinged legs making a soft, emphatic tapping. The ants, too, they say, are sick with the busyness of devouring their neighbors. They, too, must wonder if something—the Miraculous, for instance—is stirring at the periphery of their attention.

5 *Beethoven*

Downstairs, in the dim living room at five A.M., the exact hour when he slipped shoulder-, waist-, and ankle-free of his mother's body and dropped into my hands ten years ago today, my son is playing the piano, though it takes me a moment to recognize the triumphant measures of *Ode to Joy*, music by which he first understood a maker's mania, the mistaken belief that by the sheer force of one's will, a human cry may overwhelm this earth and dissolve its evil in jubilant, sacramental song.

6 *November 1989*

What a merry spectacle: patriotic anthems, raised fists, a child with a chisel, a plaza thick with a million singers, toppled statuary, tyrants in retreat. But what longed-for triumph will we celebrate next year? Or the years after that? What do we think will become of all our cherished fears, the little horrors we keep like exotic green feathers in a pouch under our ribs? The tangle of assassinations, race riots, wars of attrition, the orange robes of flame, coils of concertina wire, miles of neurotic cinder block, the severed mind, a faulted earth, techniques of crouch and cover—it was part of some miraculous purpose after all! When I was my children's age, the year between the Bay of Pigs and "Love Me Do," I woke one morning after a party, and walked through the house amazed: the furniture over-turned, the carpets covered in beer bottles and ashes, a man I did not know in his briefs passed out in the hallway. Vomit floated in the toilet. On the living room wall someone had sketched Walt Whitman's kind face with a cube of charcoal, and these words spray-painted in a red halo: "If need be a thousand shall sternly immolate themselves for one."

7 *From the Anthology of the Last Republic (I)*

Between us and boundless sky
our Maker applies His skills:
red-shifting quasars bruised into being,
clouds of cobalt and magenta gas,
stars coalescing from a bituminous void,
planets and moons like pearls of oil
smeared in a puddle, where we appear:
vague objects scumbled into being.

Our basket of hard-boiled eggs and bottles of beer
failed again to bribe the border guards,
and so, we are returning now
in the dark before day, driving
along the pot-holed road through the foothills,
pausing at a roadside shrine
to ask the Virgin of Dry Falls to forgive
the monotony of our sins.

Hope dissolved from our language
as slowly as rock salt dropped in a well
whose water is cold and black
as the skin of plums ripening in August.
Not sweet, not tart.
Rather, something always in between.
Our metaphor: above us incomparable space,
below us a factory working half-shifts,

its tall stack glittering, upwind of the city,
our valley draped in clouds of phosphorus.

The fate we were assigned.

8 *Tourism (I)*

Our friend's fiancé is showing slides of their vacation in Russia:
"Here we are in a crappy little village outside Moscow."

Click.

"Here we are at the architecturally very uninteresting gate of the Kremlin."

Click.

"Here we are waiting in yet another line."

Click.

"That is the KGB building behind us."

Click.

"Let's skip over these pictures of ourselves and the Pentecostal in his holey underwear."

Click.

"That is a Russian acrobat hanging by his hair, directly above us."

Click. Click. Click.

The images, of course, were not as he perceived them: no foreground, only the city, the horizon of concrete apartment blocks, the borders of moony, curious faces, the wide squares of the ugly socialist city. Click. And now, too, the imminent arrival of the Miraculous, and the necessary corrective: Capital Investment, the Discipline of the Marketplace!

9 *The Imperium (I)*

The "nice man" steps to the microphone: "We must not from our resolve be deterred. Demands the New World Order tireless vigilance ours! Pureness of heart ours! And yes the lives of the babies all gentle and innocent rescued from abortionists who would otherwise our great nation of its moral warriors deprive. We did not this world make this place scurvy and disastrous but we must the mantle of God's purpose accept on earth a new paradise to re-make. So in prayer let us to our Lord now our dog faces bow—"

10 *The Imperium (II)*

The jolly menace of power declares dominion. Though it loops back from its distant articulations, like Frankenstein's monster, finding its way to its maker's ancestral home. First, it infects the ghost-dancing children, the cool and ironic women, the fat and dissembling men who cannot decide what it is exactly they must do next. Finally, our fashionable detachment irradiates every molecule of creation. And neither earth—fatigued and hideous to behold—nor Hell's Bureau of Transfer can keep up with our insatiable demand for punishment to death of the guilty.

11 *Tourism (II)*

Warthogs from the nearby air base appear in tight tandems, passing low over the expressway at rush hour. The slow, thickening traffic points in a direction that leads everywhere away from the center and toward the crowded cul-de-sacs of French Glen, Riviera Estates, Avelon [sic] Meadows, in which all history is rendered benign as Europe's dream of the Golden Age. The jets divide, roll away, return one at a time to mock-strafe the grid-locked lines of luxury sedans and SUVs, then erupt skyward, the theorem for flight thrusting them toward the cloudless, near-vacuum of space miles above our daily migrations. And yet we persist like enraged salmon along a narrow corridor of concrete, inheritors of an inexplicable, always unsatisfied memory of—

12 *From the Anthology of the Last Republic (II)*
(a fragment)

Forced to project our lives elsewhere
we witnessed an all-entangling sublime
as children led hand-in-hand
under the Capitol dome,
the anniversary of the day the Senators
were stood against a wall by militiamen.

Later, with our teacher, we gathered
baskets of wild onions and mushrooms
in the forest, filled glass jars
with water from the spring where the Virgin,
raped by our enemies, bled to death, purifying us.
An inconsolable Beauty, this freedom,

impenetrable to us now as old-fashioned script
carved into stones. Our deaths came to signify
our lives, glimpses of what we were—
brief, but unbearable to look at...

13 *Of Attack*

Delirious as wrens, children dance in gravel at recess, their voices muted by gusts of wind. A woman sits alone at the kitchen table, writes, "Geraniums at the window sill sway toward the sun-lit glass," then closes her journal, and glances at the wall clock: 10:35 A.M. You pause, too, on a county road to watch flocks of white birds descend to the marsh: are they snow geese or swans? And you do not know which it is you are aware of next, because either way it is already too late: over your shoulder, four bright cylinders arcing beautifully westward across the mountains; or that sound, miles distant, the metal larynx of a siren bursting into its deconstruction of melody, a pure infantile wail of fear.

14 *The Opposition (I)*

The Pacifist pushes the lead door shut, locks himself inside his room, and mutters into his hands, "Lord of this world, forgive us what we are about to do."

15 *In the Bunker (the Movie)*

Below the Pacifist's ascetic room there is a concrete bunker lit by banks of stadium lights, the walls covered with bomb assessment photos from that "turkey shoot" along the retreat routes to Baghdad, Sarajevo, Tbilisi, Kabul, Grozny. On a big screen TV, vacant-eyed actors examine the success of this year's advances, compiling the significant lists of incidents, a montage of skinny, dark-skinned children, wounds wrapped in rags, they explain, "In some god-damned sand-nigger country, ask me if I give a fuck where." There is a rock and roll soundtrack (you would recognize all the old songs and want to sing along at the chorus). The Commandant sweats in his office, stringing a necklace of teeth for his daughter. In the auditorium, his lieutenants instruct a mob of hairy-fisted apes to hand-sign the Beatitudes.

16 *The Opposition (II)*

My masters kept me waiting, served my meal late, over-cooked, and cold, and yet I rejoice in the gift of dolphin meat! My fear recedes, and though its aroma lingers like burnt tobacco I cannot wash from my fingers, I realize now, I was not destined to live in heroic times. It is so sanitary down here in the bunker: a laundered napkin folded neatly beside my dinner plate before the blessing spoken over candles, wine, and bread. The ruin of my face glares at me from the black dinner plate, empty now but for the light of phosphorus diluted by sorrow. It was the Lord Jesus who conceived of this contradiction, this toil, this permission to love our enemies as we love ourselves.

17 *Letter to the Editor*

The Congresswoman, who insists she be called Congressman, writes: "Fellow real patriots, the time has come to either fish or cut bait. Not only our sacred Second Amendment, the right to keep and bear arms, is under assault. Many others are being abrogated. The Waco, Texas fiasco, and the Randy Weaver in Idaho. The list goes on. Who has the gold makes the rules. The UN has already begun collecting taxes in direct violation of OUR Constitution. And there are other disturbing signs. I personally saw, on my way to a miner's meeting, over two-hundred military tracked-vehicles, tanks, etc. parked on a siding. I passed another with tanks and tracked-vehicles. Ask any railroader. These movements, and also unmarked Red Army helicopters are crossing our northern borders daily. There have been strange military maneuvers in the northern States with no explanation!"

18 *From the Anthology of the Last Republic (III)*
(a fragment)

How hard how hard how hard we prayed
for the distant nest the mind makes,
a warm, woven solitude in which
our mothers felt free to sing to us
in the seamless night, seamless day,
the brilliant eighth notes of April...

19 *Romantic Ode*

A sorrowful sentimentalist raises his glass: "It will always be 1961, the handsome young president's face flickering grey at the far end of the room. My father will die in the spring and be buried under a scabby sycamore tree in Ohio. By fall, the monster Kronos will be standing in breakers just off our eastern shore, a black, menacing cylinder that blocks out the sun, its machinery humming with the inexorable evil of its economic theory. It is cold and mildewy in this cramped basement room. Sirens and klieg lights tunnel the perpetual overcast, above which our enemies float, invulnerable as gods."

20 *A Pedagogic Parable*

As she left the classroom ahead of me, a volume of Chaucer in her arms, Megumi turned and said she had not sat zazen in two weeks: "This is why I am so petulant in class!" A moment later, in the lavatory I tried to splash water on my face, but I had no face, in fact, I had no head at all! The excess skin of my neck was tucked neatly into a hole at the middle of my shoulders, clean as an infant's belly button after the stub of the knotted umbilicus rots away. I felt compelled by this odd circumstance to quiz my next class on the possibility of living without irony or guile. But they were freshmen and only stared at me in silence. Later, I tried again, with seniors, pointing to a passage from *Chronicles of the Withering State* about how we await the onset of The Extreme Event, a purifying crisis. During which everyone will lose his head, wanting to avenge himself. Of course we will brutalize our neighbors. Of course wells will be piled full of corpses that come out gray and bloated months after. And of course everyone will later feel ashamed, repentant, and not eager to ever do it again. "No, no, no! Abandon plumb and square!" By which the chronicler meant to advise us that it is always preferable to nail the mezuzah askew at the threshold, remembering to press a kiss to it with your fingers as you enter or leave. To recognize how an African weaver deliberately perplexes the perfected pattern of his design with a bright, errant thread. Or how the ceiling in the abandoned mosque (despite the Arabic precision about the mechanics of heaven) draws one's attention upward in awe of its stylized chaos, that beautiful cartoon of the mind of God. Perhaps even Megumi's odd inflection of a medieval English meter. If not these imperfect forms, headless as we are, to what else shall we bow?

21 *Whatever Happened to the Old Revolution*

A century ago, Walt Whitman, our countryman, our loyal friend, stiff and doddering from strokes, rode a train one morning west out of Denver through the mouth of Platte Canyon and steamed upward for miles to aspen groves at Kenosha Pass, where he spent an hour, declaiming "these vast and formless arrays for reasons of their own," so ecstatic at the sheer immensity of the continent that he almost forgot his train east to Camden to die.

22 *In the New World*

Grandchildren are amazed by my lies. A lush canopy of oaks sheltered these hills, narrow hollows between ridges speckled with trillium and forget-me-not. After years of drought, forests beaten away by heat, they see only grasslands edging close, a curve of unambiguous light. I was a young man when I first knew seasons had lost their pattern. That autumn, I heard a black convict executed on the radio, and later, whenever I recalled his name, Jean Françoise, I could not put out of my mind—as it was intended that I have difficulty forgetting—the crime they claim he committed in Florida. But how difficult he made it for his jailers! Confessing to nothing, refusing his meals, cigarettes, Unction. I remember picking apples after that broadcast. Remember a trip flare—the pure phosphorus of sorrow—igniting the shadow my body threw on the ground before me. And how a new caution was conceived. How deer vanished the next spring or seemed to, turning vermilion as poverty grass in famine-bleak fields.... And now the river shoals lie dry and cracked. The channel narrowed to a grassy stream. But I insist: a torpid river toiled here, thick with cadavers and silt. A dangerous current dared only by suicides and slaves who learned they were enslaved. On bluffs that once were shore, my grandchildren, suspecting nothing but lies, play a game in the ruins.

23 *From the Anthology of the Last Republic (IV) (a fragment)*

We had not yet mistaken the clock face
For the mortal course our lives may take:

Hailstones melting in sunlight,
A strange reverse-accretion of ice.

Crooked Light
(On the Archeological Discoveries from the Last Republic)

I found a fragment of deer skull tangled in weeds at my feet,
the crown between antlers, where sutures meet, the confluence
of great rivers meandering close to the brain. And as with all
skulls—of a field mouse or plover, of a porcupine or my own,
lying moss-covered beside a creek or bleached white by sun or
this one, its eye sockets threaded by bunchgrass and thistle—
these sutures are the last to come loose, reluctant to release the
fertile, knotted density they held inside. Sutures curve and curve
again, knitting together the pliant plates of the skull the way
lovers touch intricately, as grass welcomes rain after drought.
Just a blush of pink remains here along the convoluted seams,
the last glint of sun on the rippling current, afterglow of nerve-
ends firing, impulses leaping the gap, of crooked, uncontainable
light, a smoldering archaic phosphorescence that is still seeping
out like water from limestone. Even in mud of mass graves the
year after civil war ends, you will see the deliberate volunteers
tenderly cradling these inextinguishable lamps.

III

O friends, not these sounds,
but let us strike up more pleasant sounds
and more joyful!

—Friedrich Schiller

NORTH

For a quarter century, he invented it: range after range of
mountains, uplands stripped to bedrock, glaciers pouring into
fjords. The north. Cardinal point towards which he oriented
his life, though he had never found his way to its border. He
suffered the impersonality of wilderness, the dismal loneliness
of the self that occupied his fantasies. The north inhabited him
as silence inhabits a land laden with snow. He imagined a faint
trail that crossed scree to a lichen-mottled cairn at a low point
along a wind-scoured ridge. Human beings like himself had
found their way across that ridge and vanished, drifting away
to the west or south, toward the moderating influences of the
sea. But the north and its inhumanity tendrilled so deeply into
their memory, it haunts him forty generations later. Haunts him
as he bends to his knees in the garden in April to dig a row of
leeks, as the clouds spit sleet, and Berta, holding a basket, cackles
like a crow. A shocking recognition, looking up into her moss-
green eyes, migratory ghosts staring back at him, their faces and
names like his, despite the odd inflection. Signifying not his
rootlessness nor theirs, but a specific place, a clearing in a grove
of ashes, the refuge he sought at twilight a thousand years ago.

MILLENNIAL PORTRAIT, DECEMBER 31, 1999

1

One crow caws and rows the air,
an old messenger delivering a prophecy.
How shall we appease the onset of winter?
The scalding beauty of it, like a virus,
that ember of death smoldering under a rock
and carried south in saliva of a coughing child.
A chain of errors forged across a thousand years,
one link for each village our family fled.
Wolf-eyed men, fanged crossbows, blood-guttered
knives, and now that crow reminding me again:
the savage gods have not abandoned this world,
but reside here still, in its wounded fragments, the dark
our eyes can't determine the depth or texture of,
that opens and closes around us as they command.

2

In the hallucinogenic ice-fog, my sons seem
almost to shimmer in the snow-light at dusk,
though in the shapes of their faces there is a shade
of reserve, aware as they are of the odd privilege
of this glowing twilight, the incalculable probability
that we should have arrived here at all. Or remain
as late as the cold will permits, our breaths, and not
our bodies hanging in the air, our faces thrown open to sky,
as though to laugh, to protest, as though to better absorb
the moment's mortal pleasure....And now that crow
returning a third time, squawking its ironic rejoinders
about fate, about our ludicrous luck that night
our forebears—the cattle car already crammed full—
escaped into the forest and somehow survived.

FROM THE BOOK OF ESTHER

Purim comes around again, and a company of children
performs a political melodrama, fourth century B.C.,
in two acts: "Haemon's Treachery Against the Jews,"
and "The Triumph of Queen Esther."

With us tonight are two Esthers, one a visitor, a Gentile
friend of our host, and she watches and laughs, gregor in hand,
as the child who portrays her namesake asks favor
of the good King Ahasuerus.

I wipe steam from the window. It is snowing in the city,
the twelfth day of Adar, the year poised at equinox.
All is as it should be. The air in this room sweet
with schmaltz, boiled parsnips, and *knadlach*.

Queen Esther, pure of heart, always a girl crying out
to wear the crown forfeited by the royal concubine, her rival,
Vashti, who, dressed in black, we may presume was no fool
about the equation of power and sex,

Vashti, who refused the King's order to share herself
with guests at his party. And here, too, is loyal Mordecai,
Esther's kinsmen, a chubby boy who forgets his lines, whose mother
coaches him in his role as eunuch,

keeper of the harem, that his cousin, Esther, will be chosen from.
But Esther, our guest, neither pretty nor lissome,
pursued the itch of a habit, both she and her daughter beside her
infected now, chosen for the early death.

What really are we celebrating? We were taught at shul
to regard the Book of Esther as our twentieth century,
the Shoah, a metaphor of resistance:
never again.

Ahasuerus was no Hitler, but was actually Xeres, a fool
who whipped and fettered the sea, who sent away disobedient Vashti
in exchange for another whore, Esther; and Mordecai, the King's servant,
Esther's cousin, a pimp really,

simply out-maneuvered his own less ambitious rival, dim-witted Haemon.
Because of their intrigue, in Susa hundreds were slaughtered.
An ecstasy of bloodletting spread like a virus, scalded
the countryside and provincial towns.

The enmity between those two provocateurs, Haemon and Mordecai,
pretenders to the Grand Vizier, was very old, tribal, familial:
Benjaminites of the House of Saul avenging themselves
on the Amelikite clan, the Agags.

And Esther's legendary role? Allowing Agags to die
in our stead, denouncing a lecher, Haemon, who ended up
swinging from the gibbet he built for Jews.
That is what we are celebrating.

Betrayals bring us together in this aromatic room,
where the grown woman, the living Esther, remains,
no heroic abstraction, but dying—what we all fear, infected by
the shamelessness of our story.

DAVID TO BATHSHEBA

There is darker satisfaction now,
our bodies undeceived by doom,
tightening slowly, riding ecstatic swells
as though waves rolled under us
across expanses of sun-heated sea,
the whole planet's flesh rippling at our touch.

Of what consequence then is the Great Man
who long ago ordered his seal pressed
into crumbling bricks of monuments,
or the grave fire that awaits us, flames
demanding more, more mortal fuel?
Too soon, too soon

as now, after making love,
sounds return from that world on fire,
where we intrigued and deceived,
lived as though apart all day or week,
our doubles meeting at noisy banquets,
outside the temple, market square, wherever

our distracted words were spoken to no one,
words that turned back toward our mouths
appalled by our blunt indifference.
We will grow uglier, a couple of shriveled up
fools, unable even to warm ourselves
in the arms of young slaves we command.

And what other hope is there outside our time?
In erected monuments?
In traitorous Absalom? Compliant Solomon?
Or to starve with Saul in dimmest Sheol?
Bathsheba, daughter of Eliam the Hittite,
whom I made Queen of all Israel,

the logic of what I intend is not elusive:
let us dance together naked
before the ark of one true God,
and so long as we can,
in spite of our dooms,
rejoice in each other's arms.

ONE-HUNDRED SPIRALING STAIRS

One river of blood, another of cries,
a third at flood stage, full garbage and ghosts.
In such heat, error seems inevitable
as lassitude, death in an olive grove.
Her body sparkles under its thin dress
beside me, daughter of Maimonides, for whom
I ache to climb one-hundred spiraling stairs
to our room, with its one window opening
onto the shadowy warren of streets.
To enter her, linger between her hips,
her belly white as a lily against mine, kiss
the stiff, cool wells of her nipples, and come
at last together. And sleep until evening

calls us out into the plaza, where crowds
are exiting cafés, the couples leaning
and flirting at street corners. An intimate
cloud of knowing passes in a gust
acrid with the scent of sweat and oranges.
Knowing that deception neither pities
nor excuses ignorance. Exactly what
I misjudged in the Arab Quarter that day.
O city of lovers, betrayers. Rivers of blood
and cries. The grayness of fate. Of soot
gathering in bullet holes that pock stone walls.
Two furtive ghosts who kiss and clasp
through the long heat of afternoon.

CLEANSING

The woman he's about to kick in the head
is probably dead, so the young soldier, index
finger still on the trigger of his Kalashnikov,
is only elaborating one more banal
argument for the existence of God.

Or the woman is still alive, but groaning
as she dies, and this intimate sound grates
terribly on a soldier's nerves, as it means
even the power of an automatic rifle fails
to erase the pain of sentience.

And he must kick her because he heard
this same groan in his mother's room
late the night his sister was born and died,
the groan his grandmother makes each time
she sits or claws her way up from the kitchen table.

His grandmother once stole a neighbor's hen
to make him dumplings, because they envied
the neighbor's chickens that seemed
fatter, that always laid more
and richer eggs, so theft was justice.

Like a boot to the side of the head.
Like the kick of an AK and permission to use it.
Like "riddling" a body or stomping a face. Justice.
Applying himself to the cleansing of the State.
He's so happy at last, he hasn't slept for days.

AN OFFERING

Night of the Falling Stars, I dream of old Oregon,
of a series of daguerreotypes in which the Columbia
seems an inviolate blur of dunes, rapids, standing waves,
and in the background, northern forests, a smudged shadow,
a trail through the gorge disappearing into fog.

But when I wake on the fourth floor of Casita Ardilla,
the tiles beneath my bed are awash in light from Africa,
and far below, along Calle de las Maitres, my neighbor
whistles to the caged canaries who sing to him
stumbling home from the finale of La Romaría.

Wherever I wished to go along that muddy path before dawn,
I was mourning a world already lost. Those men and women
in the foreground of the daguerreotypes, lifting their nets
from that wilder river, were no longer its true subjects.
Even before the photographer's flash pot burst into chemical light,

the moment had vanished into the lush gorge behind them—
an oddly anterior future. After I dress and descend
through the spiral labyrinth of the house, I unlatch
the kitchen shutters and look out onto the blinding street,
where Antonia's mad face peers through wrought-iron,

the ghost of the dictator still haunting her misshaped body.
She reaches through the window across the blue flame of the hob,
demanding something of mine. Her open, upturned hand
every bit as immediate and appalling as one would expect,
another way of knowing how what has been will continue to be.

Into her palm I place the obligatory orange and sweaty wedge of cheese.

FERT-SPIEL WEISE

after a painting by Anselm Kiefer

A field outside of Nuremberg, the city
squatting in silhouette at the horizon. Black
towers, slate roofs of the ghetto. Sky above
pale and narrow. A scattering of clouds lit by
sun that is perpetually extinguishing itself
in the purity of the impure plains. Furrows
converge on a grove of lindens towards which
I hurry, a soiled gabardine tied at my waist
by the frayed rope I will hang myself with later.
A skim of ice, blue light of winter dusk, lies
in each trough of earth. And straw, golden straw
is strewn about the field. Not my daughter's
black hair, but fairy tale stalks the dwarf spun
into ore that still dazzles our "dark, sad eyes."
Vanity in such abundance! Enough! Enough
to sicken even a devil. O city of music,
to play is to know. Intimately as this black mud
frozen under straw, underfoot, under ice. Black,
medieval, twentieth century mud. Ignorant mud
of the circumcised and the un. Riches-at-harvest
mud. Shulamith mud. My daughter mud.
I offered her lips this dug of dry mud, "Please,"
I cried, "drink of me." It is our blood that stains
the sky. Ghosts through whose hollow gaze
you will always know a barren field. Gleaners,
nourished by blackened potatoes, moldy wheat.
Brazen and anxious as gray mice. Shadowy
tracks trailing us across the skiff of dirty snow.

TEKMERION

Remind me, someone, it's only a matter of luck
whether famine inhabits a land or not,
and infallible signs in no way prepare us for a rapture
that ruptures the small world.

If I go outside at dark to dump a bowl of Empire skins in compost
and a blue halo of ice circles the Hunter Moon,
how certain may I be that flocks of geese will form by noon
the next day, a cold rain arrive by dusk?

Bent over scythe and shears, on my knees by first light,
I cut stalks of annuals, shake out seeds,
fold perennials in protest of the coming freeze
that will outlast the night.

Let fools talk loudest who hunger for wildness,
I refuse, in October, to concede,
to unhouse my mind, and choose
to hammer larch billets a little tighter in the wood pile.

A few geese squawk above the garden,
gather into one flock, turn a last circle over the valley
and dive past Glass Hill, the customary V receding,
growing small in the south, a dark filament in a sooty sky.

Unhoused at last am I, spellbound by signs
or just the usual melancholy
of knowing we'll die before we die?
Or maybe just stubborn?

Domestic provisions don't summon much confidence,
nor does chopping away last summer's dry exuberances—
I make my prayers for the small world
to endure just one more night.

And kneeling in shelter of brittle leaves
at noon, I pick and greedily eat a few raspberries
tricked into late blossom and ripening,
even as canes rattle like death's hollow bones.

I practice my lost faith because, as I pack away my tools,
a frog peeps from its cranny in the rock wall,
and all evening, and all the next day,
a mellow rain trickles in gutters—

rain coming almost too late this year,
we feared it might not arrive,
the reservoir remain a mudflat valley of stumps,
the river a bed of algae-draped stones.

After the end of the end, if rains seem less random,
I can't imagine myself in this garden,
a man, who, no smarter nor dumber than the rest,
and neither guilty nor guiltless,

sees rocket, kale, and rainbow chard
unfold from rotten straw in March,
and fails to recognize these signs,
fails to feel unaccountably kind.

IV

Albanian Radio is asked:
Is there life on Mars?
Albanian Radio replies:
No, it's just like here.

—A popular joke

THE CARTOGRAPHER'S MELANCHOLY

Traveling south between cities, he's trying
to read, but gets stuck on one sentence:
"Finally the journey leads to the city of Tamara."

And he remembers a young woman, Tamara,
twenty-five years ago,
they met one summer, friends of a friend,

her first months in exile. She'd bribed
soldiers at the frontier,
after her city and its citizens became, not martyrs

but a sign for the capacity of people to act
with dignity and hope. All summer
he tried to seduce her, but each time they wrestled

in the dark, she pulled away and said sorry,
she couldn't. Soon, she left
to become an oil geologist, and then he departed,

beginning an unremarkable life that led to this
train, this annotated history
of phantom capitals open on his lap, absorbed

in his sour regrets—not Tamara's absence,
but his own, how
melancholy, and not a man, occupies his seat.

On page thirteen, in blocky script in the margin
the first owner of his book wrote:
"We are residue of delinquent desires."

Past the glass of the air-conditioned coach,
sun bleaches basin and foothills
blonde as Tamara's hair that evening she said

she'd no longer see him, apologized
and shut the door.
He walked to the corner, caught a metro bus

a quarter century ago, then this commuter train,
on which he feels poised again
at the verge of dormant life, a parallel geography—

where expectancy and phantoms permit us to live
multiple lives in concurrent times.
But why? Why bedazzle us with the invisible

grinding to frustrated stasis at the middle of each?
What disappoints him
is the absurd calculus of fates—how their lives,

Tamara's and his, might coincide again, that,
for instance, tomorrow
she will pass a café at noon as he twists lime into beer,

and as he thinks something inane like citric acid burns one's cuticles,
they will glance at each other
blankly, and look away because this is stupid

fantasy, a middle-aged hypochondria, a weightless
existence in marginalia.
Parenthetically: "(None of us exist.)"

HAVENS

The cold descends from the north
and all the spaces between us fill up
with silence, as in the spaces between voices
in a cantata that comes on the radio
at dawn, a calming segue between
morning's first cycle of news and the next.

In our bleak kitchens, fluorescent lights
sputter with grief, and the coffee cup
brims with a sour chill. Stunning,
on the best days in winter,
how quickly we abandon that uneasy
dream of a self we cannot account for.

Who were we, touching those shapes
of affections that seemed intimate
as a woman's sorrow? That child
at the river, trying to hold water in her arms?
That man, who longed to ply
downward into the dark solitudes of soil?

Before we opened our eyes,
we opened eyes that were like tiny opals
and hurried along the discursive paths
our confidants, the field mice, plowed
under layers of snow, so we might guess
the way from one nest to the next, our soul's

remote, half-remembered tenancies on earth.

VOYEURISM

Heather was majoring in mathematics with a minor in philosophy, and had just separated from John, the father of her infant daughter, because he wanted so much more to become a rock star than a father. Her classmates were mostly girls, recent graduates of high school proms, and bewildered boys, ballcaps secreting callow eyes. Mostly, they chose to ignore Heather as one a little older than themselves, who had forged ahead, in error and not inevitably, into a territory where they were sure they wouldn't tread. I repeated my question a third time, and they sat there staring back, dazed, lost, until Heather, who seemed agitated, answered with a strange intensity foreign to those who nurse amnesia. She'd seen a TV report of women waiting in line to claim the bodies of daughters in tight jeans and t-shirts, and the bodies of their toddler sons, stripped to their briefs, all lying together in neat ranks on the floor of a morgue. Another ordinary scene from a city under siege, bombed, mortared, sniped, and starved. And Heather said she felt ashamed. Ashamed? Yes, we participate. Outraged and hurt but unable to act, we either switch channels or worse watch, fascinated, full of sentiment. She switched channels, but still couldn't touch her daughter. Even though the child cried for milk until Heather's breasts ached and wept. She just stared out the window at herds of deer crossing vacant lots behind her subsidized apartment. The deer, she said, made her sick with irony, this privilege of being witness to what she can't change, and that gives the lie to an ethical life. But it was too late to continue, a minute after the hour, her classmates zipping up their packs to leave.

GNOSIS

1

She carried on about her failure too long. It leaned
precariously at the middle of the studio,
a rickety, re-constructed chest of drawers
high on a mound of mirrors she smashed,

her *Book of Revelations*.
Inside of it she had carved and painted
faces from the myth of her childhood. Not once,
she complained, because she knew the difference,

had the *Book* carried her beyond its mundane making,
a longed-for flight, the dissolution of self
in the grace of—

and here,
she struggled for the proper word.

2

Another student, at the far end of the studio,
took a piece of charcoal in his left hand,
the right hand deformed, and began
to sketch an ecstatic Jesus, the Savior's face

open as a child's, laughing at the follies of Thomas.
But in the corner of the paper, emptiness
demanded he bring it into being, a point of intimacy
where he must reveal the Son of God's hand

reaching toward us, open and generous.
And fascinating to watch, like a striptease,
wondering, How far will it go?

Not far, of course.
With his grotesque hand he rubbed it all out.

3

We might have left that room sooner, gone out
into the streets, joined other people heading home
after work, dissolved into snowy twilight
and soon, shared a drink, and another night of forgetting.

I, too, have failed now, forgetting
my own bafflement at the predicament
of bringing forth whatever is in us
before we destroy it

because of a flaw
that exists in the world, in ourselves,
so that it seems we are driven by ghosts,

by sheer ignorance and pretense,
destined to fail just shy of becoming
        greater amplitudes of love.

HEROIC POSE

1

He knew it would be his final visit to Herschelstraat.
And he would have to hurry to catch the last tram from Oost
to his room near the havens, where dusk lingered after midnight,
and crowds in the station were still bright with students
arriving from every nation of the world, young men and women
troubled only by the undiscovered islands of each other's flesh.
He walked among them, convinced that his friend, Tina,
remained the same vivid, principled young woman
as when they arrived there, too, twenty-five years ago,
though he knew she was a ruin now, shriveled up to thirty kilos,
hands curled to claws, her voice rough as a jackdaw's.
Whatever it was that once was Tina, he swore (he loved and lied)
still filled that room on Herschelstraat as he focused the camera lens.

2

What the lens found in Tina's face was impossible for him to see,
until, in the cramped darkroom in the seventh year
of her lying in twilight between two worlds, she appeared
in the white tray before him, a ghost caught in warm jellies of emulsion,
the grainy image he exposed because a camera won't fail, as he had,
to see in a fraction of a second, in an isolated room along a side street
in a city half the world distant from the city of her birth
how Tina alone suffered, kept awake by the despairing hum
of machinery that kept her alive. By the time he saw this,
she had gone mad, covered with sores, tied to bed-rails
so as not to convulse, claw her brittle skin, beg for
death. And her lover tormenting her as he was tormented,
refusing, as loyalty requires, the offer of rescue.

3

It's a heroic pose, how she willed to be seen now,
eyes gray with blindness, the acid grimace that was her smile.

A FLEMISH JAY
for Gooitzen Zwanenburg

North wind dense with the scent
of Polder and salt, and the old
filth of Amsterdam, I kneel
at the gate to Vondelpark,
pick up a molted scapular,
count alternating ribbons of color
that camouflaged a bird,
brushstrokes so unfaltering
I know every student
must study this same master—
black fading to darkest blue to
a filament of white, black again,
then blue, and again white,
repeated nineteen times
along the shaft of the quill—
that small, cast aside feather!

A Flemish jay, my friend says.
In the havens, wooden ships begin
rocking on choppy waves,
but the mind yields, porous
as pumice, absorbing the radiant
present, in which the name suddenly
steadies the body that otherwise
would mourn an absence,
evidence of loss, of flight. I pinch
the feather between my fingers.
Will carry it across the pack ice
above the Pole. So as not to stray
from this privileged moment, this
stubborn resilience of language
already turning inward, making it
lovely, and almost whole.

PERSEIDS

She invited me to the lake one night to watch meteors shower upon
our upturned faces, an offer of "a once in a lifetime celestial event"
that never occurred. Only a few bright stragglers skidded across the sky,
though at the velocity of falling bodies, burning up to nothing.

By April, that young woman would be turned out of town by rumor—
an adulteress, a whore. But that August night, the meteor shower
having failed, she opened the long, wide barrel of a telescope,
turned the lens toward the southwest to show me—brilliantly

present there in the dark, tilted on its axis—Saturn, the austere
god of demarcations, rings so precisely etched on the polished mirror,
for a moment I stopped scheming about that young woman,
grew dizzy, began stumbling into the emptiness between

the unspeakable beauty of the object and its reflection,
a boundary I knew language will never cross, even as distance
closed around me. An improbable intimacy. This was a decade ago.
And now I've forgotten her first name, whose smooth face joined mine

at the mirror, and just once brushed my lips, almost lightly as a word.

OF WATER

There's neither two nor three.
Because the dying still wander from the blast zone.
Because you may "visit," where.
Because of the student.
Because of the city.
Because there's an island in the river, where.
Because the dying still lie in a grove of trees.
Because I don't know the names of the trees.
Because the trees, too, are a presence.
Because the student folds a chain of paper cranes.
Because in the photograph she points to.
Because of the sound of water.
Because they sing, "O, quickly, quickly now."
Because they sing.
Because the sky inhabits the skeletal dome.
Because they shave the collaborator's head.
Because she goes mad.
Because in the name of peace, the park, where.
Because of *Himmel und Erde*.
Because, "Forgive me, I must pole your punt across."
Because she leaves origami cranes.
Because she leaves them in our names.
Because the dying raise their heads.
Because an invisible hand steadies them.
Because of the unreality of light, its apocalyptic absence.
Because when we offer a drink.
"Of water?" "Of water, yes."
We bow. In shame. In gratitude.

AND THE PURSUIT OF HAPPINESS

Why reclining? why myself and all drowsing?
What deepening twilight—scum floating atop the waters,
Who are they as bats and night-dogs askant in the capitol?
                              —Whitman, "To the States"

Below the turbines at Bonneville Dam
the Gorge walls released the river to wide flats,
and FM radio crackled back to life, the aerial pulling in
a broadcast of old songs from a time (so a popular notion goes)

when young people united against the cunning lies of the State
that conspired, as always, to lull its citizens to sleep—
music that typically irritates me with its demands
grown cozy and benign now as advertising copy.

But somehow not irritating yesterday.
To what endangers us, there seems no other possible response
than impolitic songs that share one assumption:
our own excess terrifies us. I wasn't really thinking

much farther ahead than the next bend in the river,
just one moment tumbling into another, music
radiant and sad as it seemed decades ago when I heard it
as a child during the war, when the entire nation seemed

to shake itself awake and declare, *No. Not this. Enough.*
The duration of a song, too, might deliver my sons—
who sat side-by-side in the front seats and directed us at 80 mph
toward the coast—to safety, might lead them across the pass

I crossed with men my age, to reach that point when skepticism
makes us unfit to be soldiers of a corporate state. Despair,
it seemed, evaporated in those old songs, or despair
condensed into a heavier substance, a grim resolve.

Hours later, we left our room and walked a path
through forests to Highway 101, then, crossing,
dodged headlights, and crested the grassy headland
above the beach, stepped past the glow of a soda machine

so our eyes could adjust to blackness of sea and stars
swarming out of bounds from far horizon to near,
half the dome of heaven, eternity spinning away,
whichever way we turned—except for turning down

to the beach, where bonfires like orange beacons stretched
along that narrow filament of coast, fires lit by a thousand families,
who, for a moment belied despair. Some were even singing.
And this morning, too, the tide going out, we found ourselves

among thousands more—all walkers, kite-fliers and kissers,
children burying each other in sand, or sad bastards
finding pleasure just sitting alone and staring off
at some painful particular no one else seemed aware of,

or surfers flopping backwards off their boards, or two Goths
staring into handfuls of water, where shadows of sand shrimp
(the colorful, opaque entrails of an otherwise invisible body politic!)
jittered across their opens palms, enough happiness their black lips

almost smiled—people just goofing off in the fog closing around us,
so that all the water, stacks of basaltic rocks and headlands
glowed as though we had drunk a sweet narcotic
and saw ourselves and earth coated in a permanent rime of gold.

August 2002

V

The present distribution of mountains and rivers, of fields, of meadows, of steppes, of forests and seashores, cannot be considered final.

—*Leon Trotsky*

INDIRECTIONS

The blustery dark before day. Storms toiling toward shore.
Rain giving the house its familiar shape—the pitch
of a mossy roof, a windward wall that heaves and creaks.
You keep checking the clock. Oatmeal bubbles in its pot.
In the window glass, a distorted face. Already, you have forgotten
what time it is. When you grow old, you will knot bright ribbons to
familiar things—surveyor's flags, orienting the territories of loss.

*

The swell rising off shore, some far place where mind
is general as wind, not this focused blast that strips
windward limbs from spruces, prunes to the trunk.
It is important not to believe too soon you understand
what you think you see.
                         The shore, too,
is one of the tragic edges between intimacy and distance.

*

What is distance, that it could be understood as less
complex than separation in time or space? More. A trail
through old growth, a cathedral silence now after surf
tapers to a small, ambient complaint, slipping under the sound
a creek makes as it finds its way over polished cobbles,
hurrying this last mile to the beach, where the freshet
braids across sand and shingle, giving itself back to sea.

*

Your own thought returns, too, though your body remains
this mile inland.
                  A dozen changed rivulets, redefined by the reach
of each wave, and always this fresh water from mountains
mixing with salt at the shore. Though before solution occurs
there is this moment, as much an edge as any other, when
what has traveled as far as a lifetime remains distant,

*

immeasurably apart.
You had intended only a slow hour's walk inland, stopping to stare
at the mossy slope, at broken spruces, at rotted trunks
fifteen feet wide at the base, and the young—call them young—
a second generation three-hundred years old, who refuse to let go
of those rich seed beds of russet flesh.
        Soft and resilient, but cold, too, as fate.

*

Children behind you on the trail shake down pink drops of rain
beaded on the flowering branches of salmonberry. Cold
on the bare neck. They play a game, hiding, crouched in the dark
beneath exposed roots of one of those behemoth trees
where the host tree rotted away beneath, leaving a damp room
lit by moss-light,
        an intimacy they misunderstand?

*

Intimacy that you found yourself wishing for once
as a younger man, wandering in a timbered canyon,
astonished by what you had seen many times:
        an old broken fir on the ground,
a dense grove of saplings sprouting from the host,
the dead speckled by orchids, lichens, and lilies, older and
younger than you were then, blending into drifts of forest slough.

*

Here is that legendary stink again:
heavy spring snow flopping off limbs
onto skunk cabbage, onto orange and yellow fungi,
fruiting in the perpetual shade.
Every year of your life you are drawn down
to the low places, regions of muck and rot,
of quicksand and slime, stench of continuous afterbirth.

*

Because you are seeking welcome in the canyons,
in the walnut-shell intimacy that enfolds you,
because, despite the familiar saltiness of blood kissed many times
from your cut fingertips,
                    because you feel inadequate for the sea,
because your footing is steady, earth-firm
you dare neither rip-tide nor undertow.

                    *

Children dared the Angel,
                    slipped out of their clothing
and dove into cold surf. Seals, who do not suffer
because of the sea, watched impassively from the rookery,
as those children washed ashore, laughing, alive.
Death did not want them yet, because
they were stupid or miraculously adequate for the sea.

                    *

The freshet surges across the beach to be consumed by.

After the horned moon appears, spring tides retreat farther from.

A city carved from dense basalt, a mile beyond.

It is incomplete. It is not a city.

It is the sand flea's way to eat words from a page.

And these shadows young shrimp cast, despite transparent bodies.

Surely there is an easier way to lose your mind.

                    *

Always this limit to what you believe you understand.
Be grateful.
                    All curves are subtle, deceiving, difficult to perceive:

you crossed a mountain ridge, unaware that the trail had looped back
in the opposite direction, and nothing could convince you otherwise,
not the sun as it flared from clouds and set where it rose
nor rose again from clouds, out over the ocean, only a mile west.

　　　　　*

Who could sleep in such a place?
　　　　　Better that the ocean lie
where it belongs a mile west, early sun in the east again,
briefly warming your shoulder.
　　　　　When you step away from the creek
rain hisses in the deep canopy, the surf at high tide,
squalls driven ashore ahead of a gale spawned from the nest of storms.

　　　　　*

Wind is coming home in a hurry from the far edge of a sphere.

A child, spinning in wet sand, draws a circle with a stick.

Or the child's father, a giant gyrating.

An aggressive urge to punish what is younger than wind.

Xeres whipping and fettering the waves!

Chunks of young basalt, breaking away from the continent.

And the young slumping forward into waves, closing the distance.

　　　　　*

Wind and waves are finale of distance,
cutting inland wherever they decide, hard
as the continent's edge.
　　　　　You step back scared
and stumble on rough lava, breakers
spouting and spraying a cold, fishy mist.　The Devil's Churn.

Finale of distance. Ending.

*

Recurring: again:
you cheered the violent surge, turned your back to the abrupt
edge of the cape, waves rising over the reefs a mile out,
waves rising high over your head—you turned your back!
Bowed to the green and purple anemones, bowed to red stars,
to kelp and sea grass, to barnacles crunching underfoot,
to stacks of oysters in dense swirls, clinging in sheltered pools.

*

A maze of rocks below headlands. Tide out as far as its turning back.

A city. Not a city.

Narrow alleys. Not narrow alleys drifted with sand.

Empty at this hour for ten thousand years. Rows of darkened houses.

Knock on stone. Knock on stone.

For their jewels, jeering soldiers offered crusts of bread. For jewels.

Children yell to hurry back. There are garnets in the creek.

*

The wealth of the city washes from a cliff above the empty streets.
You pick through the stones, hold one to the light
that makes its way through stone as though from a great distance.
                    Above you,
a headland layered with buried midden heaps of white shells,
caves large enough for you to stand in out of the rain, wilderness
tumbling down from slovenly hills. The city awaiting its daily invasion.

*

And she is trapped in this city, too.
                        The spider smothered in her gooey silk,
struggling to retract the thread, the sweet protein
she spun from her own weightless substance,
intricate design of infinitesimal mind.
Like an acrobat:
                        see how she hangs from her hair?

                        *

A surf that rough draws every face to the window glass to peer
even into the dark, catching perhaps no more than the image
of ghosts staring back.
                        A fragment of moon,
                        a planet floating
in the calm above the ragged squalls, a sliver
of light riding the waves all the way along the beach.

                        *

A legion of snakes, rivulets of spray uncoiling across saltgrass,
old cedar stumps ripped up from their roots
and large as grizzlies lumbering toward us out of the surf.
The young squeal at the thought, rush away to hide in the back rooms,
the older children laughing nervously.
                        Rain and wind batter the four walls.

Lord of this world, forgive us our lives, our losses, their erratic shapes.